Michigan's
Most Haunted

A Ghostly Guide to the
Great Lakes State

Sandy Arno Lyons

Manufactured in the United States of America.
Copyright 2007

Edited by: Dr. Susan Richardson
Photographers: Steven Oatley & Sandy Arno Lyons
Layout/Photo Consultant: Steven Oatley
Cover Design/Baldwin Illustrations: Tom Zahner of Curve Detroit

SkateRight Publishing
First Edition 2007

Library of Congress Control Number: 2007906168

ISBN 978-0-9798876-0-4

Acknowledgments:

A special thanks to everyone that willingly took part in this exciting project. Without you this book would not have been possible.

Specifically:

Anton, Anton's Publishing Primer

Amy & Tom, CurveDetroit.com

Steven Oatley, www.Axisfilms.tv

David, D&R Paranormal Investigations

Julie, The Sweet Dreams Inn

Patty & Angela, The Terrace Inn

The Murphys, Murphy's Lamplight Inn

Chrissy, George, Christine & Kim,
        Holly Hotel

Steve & Kathie, LaSalle-Griffon
        Organization

Barbara, The National House Inn

David, Perry Hotel

Lesley, Scott & Doug, Baldwin Theatre

A Few Words of Thanks:

To my amazing parents, Barb and Mike Arno, and my sister, Amy MacIntosh, for listening to all my crazy ideas and never letting me give up on my dreams.

To my loving husband, Chris, for being the current recipient of my crazy ideas and for supporting me no matter what.

To my students at Figure Skating Club of Birmingham and Berkley Royal Blades Figure Skating Club for allowing me to do what I love: you inspire me every day.

Dedicated to those in search of the unknown

"I see dead people"
The Sixth Sense, 1999

"I ain't afraid of no ghost"
Ghostbusters, 1984

I wasn't sure which quote was more appropriate. What can I say? I'm a believer with a sense of humor.

Table of Contents

Foreword

I have always enjoyed a good tale. Growing up I pursued anyone who had something to say about things never taught in school nor written down. After spending the past 10 years reading other Michigan ghost books by Marion Kulco, Dan Asfar and Rev. Gerald Hunter, just to name a few, I was inspired to write my own. The stories I encountered are such gems that they needed to be told and the places made public. People should be able to visit and decide for themselves whether to believe or not.

Obviously, none of these stories can be proven scientifically, but I can assure you these stories are true to the best of the participants' knowledge. I only included stories that were interesting and given to me by reasonable, sane and sober people. I had to sort through a lot of old wives' tales, obvious hoaxes and childish nonsense before finding the real jewels. Everyone had some story of random dish rattling or unexplained bumps in the night.

Whenever possible, I've traveled to local libraries, museums and spoken with many a historian to check facts. One of the problems is deaths at hotels and

1

restaurants are not publicized for obvious reasons. And, as anyone who has researched genealogy will tell you, death records are organized by date and name, not place. Restaurants don't record customer names, and old hotel guest registries are usually long gone.

In conducting the various interviews and visiting all the properties for this book, I have made the following observations:

1) Ghosts don't necessarily haunt the places where they died. They haunt the places that they visited in life. And, in many cases, they haunt their favorite places: vacation spots and social hangouts.

2) Three things need to be present for ghostly activities:

> • Sensitive individuals who can pick up on slight shifts in energy levels. Not everyone has this trait and "seeing is believing."

> • A quiet and relaxed atmosphere so that energy can more easily be detected, hence why sightings usually occur at night.

> • An older property with original architectural features. This is why occurrences are usually found in older parts of buildings.

It may come as a shock to find out that I've never actually seen a ghost, which is a good thing—I scare easily. What I have noticed about the places I've visited is that the air seems heavier, not with humidity, but with a little extra something, like energy, which isn't present at my house—Thank God!

Maybe you have a tale to tell or have information on the people or places presented in this book. Any new information that can help substantiate stories or provide more details will be included in future editions of this book.

Also I'm always looking for more haunted B&B's, restaurants, pubs, theaters, stores, etc. I stay away from private residences—Who would want their address publicized? I avoid graveyards—need I say more? And I run like hell away from anything too creepy or evil—otherwise, I'd be up all night worried that the clown from *Poltergeist* is going to find me.

Email me your stories, findings or new leads to sandy.lyons@yahoo.com.

I hope you have as much fun reading and visiting the places in this book as I did researching and writing this book.
Happy Hauntings,
Sandy

The Ones That Got Away

Allegan, Michigan
Upscale restaurant, just outside of town:

According to the internet, they're haunted by a lumberjack who died on the property. One employee said, "Oh yeah, we're definitely haunted." The manager did not return any of my five phone calls.

Near Muskegon
Upscale restaurant and inn, just outside of town:

I sent them my standard "Are you interested in being in my book?" email in May [2007]. A month later I visited their website to get their phone number to follow up on my original inquiry. As it turns out, just two weeks after I sent my email, the entire place was destroyed by fire. Thank God, no one was injured. Very sad.

Oxford, Michigan
A bar on main street, downtown:

Rumor has it that the bar has an old slave tunnel in the Michigan basement haunted by a Civil War soldier. Employees confirmed something weird was going on, but the manager said, "I have no idea what you're talking about." After that, employees' memories seemed to fade really fast. Hmmmmm.

Westland, Michigan
Former tavern near an old saw mill:

The internet details how an old mill worker was killed in a freak accident and haunts the property. The report went on to say that ghost-hunting investigations showed a picture of his face in ectoplasm, whatever that means. My email inquiry was answered immediately by a very polite individual who said, "This just isn't our kind of thing." (But having ghost busters run around with an ectoplasm machine is? Whatever.)

Sweet Dreams Inn
Victorian Bed & Breakfast

Bay Port, Michigan

bayportchamber.com   **(989) 656-9952**

History

    The Sweet Dreams Inn was built in 1890 by William H. Wallace as his personal residence. He and his family lived on the first and second floors. The third floor was a large ballroom and featured wood floors and vaulted ceilings. According to local historians, every Saturday night Mr. Wallace hosted large parties with music and dancing that lasted until morning.

Sweet Dreams Inn   Bay Port, MI

William H. Wallace founded and operated a successful rock quarry business and dabbled in local politics. This enabled him to build and own many of the properties that surrounded his home, including the massive Bay Port Hotel that once occupied the waterfront across the street. A stage coach stop located near the old hotel brought travelers from all over.

The house remained in the Wallace family for nearly 100 years until Betty Rapson purchased the property and turned it into a bed & breakfast in the 1980's. Two years later it sold again and, with the new owner, came additional improvements and personal touches.

Renovations made in the mid 1980's included adding bathrooms to each bedroom by removing the secret passageways that connected all the rooms on the second floor. Speculation as to what these secret passageways were used for has run the gamut from maids' entrances to prohibition bootleg operations.

In July 2001 Julie Chaperon purchased the building and changed the name to the Sweet Dreams Inn. She believes that the strange-shaped closets on the third floor

The back of each closet, throughout the third floor, turns into a long and narrow space.

could still be connected via small crawl spaces.

　　Current renovations and remodeling have prevented further inspection of these cramped spaces. Unexplained activities prevent many guests from completing their overnight stay.

Ballroom Blitz

The Rose Room always had stories of doors shaking, personal items being moved and lights being turned on and off. "It never really bothered me; it just seemed rather innocent. It's like whoever lived here before is still here," Julie, the owner, said.

Many of her guests, however, did not feel the same way. Over the years, many guests staying in that room have exited in the middle of the night without any explanation. "I knew why!" Julie said. "They just couldn't handle it."

Two of the owner's friends, Kim and Anne, were about to have an experience of their own. In the fall of 2003, the pair were sleeping in the Rose Room on the second floor. Julie, the owner, her daughter, and a friend were sleeping on the third floor.

In the middle of the night, the two sleeping in the Rose Room were awakened by what seemed to be a loud party above them on the third floor. They could hear people laughing and talking and loud music. They could even hear furniture being moved over a wood floor. The music was odd too; it was very old music, not oldies,

but chamber or ballroom music from
the 1900's.

The pair were confused. It was late
and the sounds were so loud. They went
upstairs to find out what was going on.
Upon reaching the third floor, everything
got quiet. Opening the door on the third
floor, they saw everyone sleeping and no
signs of a party.

"Well, that's strange," they both
thought. They headed back downstairs,
and as soon as they got into bed, the party
started up again in full swing. "Well,
whatever it is, at least they're having fun!"
they said. The party lasted all night and
ended only when the sun came up.

**The third floor, formerly a ballroom,
was renovated in the 1980's into a
large suite with carpeted floors.**

Girls' Weekend

In winter 2004 the current owner, Julie, and her daughter, April, invited several of their friends over for a much needed girls' weekend. After a good meal and hours of girl talk, Nikki, one of April's friends, was tired so she excused herself from the dining room and headed to bed.

Everyone assumed she went upstairs to go to bed. They heard her walk up the stairs and shut the door. As time went on, more and more noise was coming from the second floor. It sounded like children laughing and running up and down the halls. Unusual, they thought, for someone who was so tired.

Finally at 2 am, becoming tired themselves, they went to go tell Nikki to knock it off. As they started to climb the stairs, they noticed the parlor doors on the first floor were shut.

Julie opened the parlor door only to find Nikki sleeping. Nikki, who woke up when the door squeaked open, asked, "Is everything OK?"

Stunned, Julie asked her, "Have you been sleeping in here all night?"

Nikki, half asleep, said, "Yeah, why?"

Julie asked, "Did you go upstairs at all?"

Nikki replied, "No, why?"

"No reason. Go back to sleep," Julie said quietly before shutting the door.

By this time, the rest of the group had figured out what was going on and got really scared. "If Nikki was downstairs this entire time, who's upstairs?" Kim, one of Julie's friends, asked with a shaky voice.

Julie didn't know what to say. Her friends were obviously very upset, and she didn't want to make them feel worse by detailing all the unexplained events on the second floor.

All of the bedrooms have a guest diary where visitors can record their experiences. The one in the Rose Room has disappeared.

Sweet Dreams Inn   **Bay Port, MI**

Kim and some of the others were nearly crying and started to pack their things—they'd had enough. It was 2 am, but they wanted to leave.

Julie, who was now really worried about her friends, yelled upstairs, "Stop It! I mean it. Stop it!" and the noise from the second floor ceased.

Eventually, Julie calmed everyone down and convinced them to stay. All was quiet for the rest of their stay. Although Julie is still friends with everyone who visited that weekend, some of them, like Kim, have never returned to the Sweet Dreams Inn.

Stagecoach Travels

Autumn is a beautiful time all across Michigan, especially in Bay Port, where the large trees burst into their famous foliage. Contrast this with the background of green grass and the sun still reflecting off the lake, and you can see why people flock here.

Two guests of the Sweet Dreams Inn were enjoying a relaxing visit and admiring the beautiful autumn colors. The fall hues were not the only thing they saw during their visit.

It was fall of 2005, and the pair were sitting on the large wraparound porch of the Sweet Dreams Inn. The sun had set hours earlier, and the night air was cool and crisp. Since the inn is a smoke-free establishment, they were outside enjoying a smoke.

As they relaxed on the porch enjoying the peace and quiet, the sound of horses broke the evening silence. Off in the distance, on the road, they could see a stagecoach come into view. It was a misty, shadowy image of horses pulling a coach. After a few seconds the image vanished.

Sweet Dreams Inn   Bay Port, MI

The stunned guests looked at each other. After confirming they both saw the same thing, they dashed inside and relayed their story to the owner, Julie, who was intrigued but not surprised.

Julie joked with her good-natured guests, who were quite amused at the experience. "Well, at least this time, it's outside!" Julie laughed.

This stone pile, identified by a green historical marker, is all that remains of a stagecoach stepping stone that once led to the old Bay Port Hotel. It's located just down the street from the Sweet Dreams Inn.

Terrace Inn
Bay View, Michigan

theterraceinn.com   **(800) 530-9898**

History

Originally opened in 1911 in the heart of Bay View, Michigan, the Terrace Inn is the only year-round bed & breakfast in a seasonal community. Bay View, which is only open from May-November, began as a Methodist camp in 1875.

The 438 Victorian summer homes on the Bay View grounds are meticulously maintained to retain their original grandeur. The Terrace Inn features turn-of-the-century transoms, tall ceilings and original 1900's glass. Inside, the feeling continues with odd-shaped closets, wide verandahs and a few original guests.

Hallway Happenings

In the winter of 2005, a guest, Francie, staying on the second floor was asleep in her room. At 3 am she was awakened by voices just outside her room. A middle-aged woman was talking, laughing and seemingly saying good night to her party chums. Then Francie heard a door shut firmly.

Annoyed, she figured it was just other guests being rude in the middle of the night. As she tried to go back to sleep, she remembered that it was the off season at the inn, and she was the only one staying in that part of the building.

Forty minutes later, it was the same situation all over again—loud voices from the hallway. The same middle-aged woman was saying good night to her friends, and then the door shut. It was as if the entire conversation completely repeated itself.

Francie, irritated, got up and looked outside her door. No one was in the hallway, and all the other doors were open, just as they were when she went to bed.

Terrace Inn   Bay View, MI

Francie tried to go back to sleep, but something about what the woman said, twice, stuck out in her mind. Her words seemed so out of context for modern-day vocabulary. Although she couldn't remember exactly what the woman said, it was something like, "Good night, my friends, until morning's first light."

Francie stayed in Room 212, which is located in the oldest part of the inn.

The next morning Francie further inspected the other rooms in the hallway. All the doors were open, and rooms were completely vacant.

Christian Rock Rules!

In the summer of 2006, Angela was the night manager at the Terrace Inn. Her duties included working by herself at night to prep for breakfast the following day. "It was always a night manager's goal to finish before 1[am] 'cause that's when things happened," she said.

The kitchen, on many occasions, had given Angela and other staff members the feeling that someone was watching—especially after midnight.

Staff members describe an overwhelmingly male presence that just seemed to be staring. "It was unnerving, but I still had work to do," Angela said. She coped with the lonely job and the weird feelings by playing Christian music to lighten the mood in the empty kitchen.

On this particular night she decided to change things up a little and play some country music. It was a catchy tune, and she quickly settled into her work.

At about 10:30 out of the corner of her eye, she saw a dark, shadowy figure dart around her. Angela said, "It whizzed by me so quickly that it almost touched me. I even felt a breeze like you

21

would feel if someone ran by you."

This time she was more than unnerved. She was scared and had a really bad feeling. "I immediately switched the music back to Christian rock and said a prayer," she said. "I felt better and was able to finish my work."

Although she still gets a strange feeling in the kitchen, she never saw the dark figure again. "Anytime I have to work in the kitchen alone at night, I always have Christian music playing," she said.

The kitchen is located behind the dining room in the oldest part of the building.

Calming Presence

Angela, former night manager of the Terrace Inn, still helps out at the inn from to time doing everything from housekeeping to kitchen duties. Often she would be in the basement tending to the laundry.

Occasionally she would notice a white Victorian gown floating in the middle of the laundry room. Sometimes she would see it out of the corner of her eye, and other times it would be right in front of her. No one was wearing the dress; it just seemed to be floating by itself. "Then it would slowly fade away," she said.

It was a very calming female presence. "Either that or it was a cross-dressing ghost!" she laughed. All in all, she felt protected. "I definitely felt like someone was watching out for me, like a mother would watch over her child," she continued.

The presence was the complete opposite of the feeling she got in the kitchen (see previous story). In fact, she would prefer to be in the laundry room rather than any other part of the basement, especially the dry storage room.

Terrace Inn   Bay View, MI

For years employees would avoid the dry storage room. It's a weird little room, rectangular in shape. Doing laundry one afternoon and needing bleach, Angela marched into the room. She suddenly felt and overwhelming and scary presence. Afraid, she quickly grabbed the bottle of bleach and jolted out of the room. Then she heard the sound of breaking glass— twice. She was completely alone.

Once back in the laundry room, she felt relieved. Although she didn't see the white gown this time, she felt a calming presence. "I just knew everything was going to be OK," she sighed.

The narrow door in the back of the dry storage room leads to an old boiler closet.

Murphy's Lamplight Inn
Central Lake, Michigan

murphyslamplight.com   **(231) 544-6443**

History

Built in 1924 by local stone masons, the hotel WE-GO-TA, as it was called, featured 22 rooms and four bathrooms. For years the train brought vacationers, traveling salesmen and those looking for an overnight before heading further north to Mackinaw or the Upper Peninsula.

Murphy's Lamplight Inn Central Lake, MI

Over the years the property changed owners and names. Each time the new owners put their own stamp on the place by making renovations and by shifting the focus from lodging to food to a happening bar scene. In the 70's Doug and Mary Lou Denny purchased "The Palace," changed the name to the Lamplight Inn and converted it into a bed & breakfast. In the 80's the Strzempeks bought the property, closed the bed & breakfast and brought back fine dining.

In early 1996 Mary Ellen Murphy, on a weekend getaway from Dearborn, Michigan, saw that the Lamplight was for sale, and soon her entire family called Central Lake their home. Personalizing the property, she renamed it Murphy's Lamplight Inn, and features fine dining and spirits. Two kinds of spirits are offered here—the kind that are served with dinner and the kind that are often seen roaming the property.

Murphy's Lamplight Inn   Central Lake, MI

Lady in White

During the 1980's the owner at the time was painting on the second floor when he saw a young woman in a bridal gown. Confused, he asked, "What are you doing here?" She turned and ran down the hall. The man chased her but stopped in his tracks when she disappeared as she ran straight through a stack of boxes.

The entire second floor has been remodeled many times.

One rumor says that a daughter of a former hotel manager was preparing to elope with her fiancee but tripped on her wedding gown while descending the ladder. Research is ongoing to determine the origins of this story. At the time of printing, it could not be substantiated.

Murphy's Lamplight Inn   Central Lake, MI

Little Girl Lost

Over the years customers, workers and owners have seen a little girl roaming the halls on the second floor. She playfully peeks out the bedroom doors into the hallway. People often ask, "Is that your daughter?" They are shocked to find out she's not real.

Dressed in Victorian garb with long, dark, curly hair, she appears to be 7 or 8 years old. Just like any other child she runs, plays, laughs and seems to like animals. The owner's late dog, Lacey, was a great dog, but she was "a little crazy," Mary Ellen, the owner, said. Lacey was often seen playing alone on the second floor, jumping, rolling and barking as if a child was playing with her.

One of the owner's daughters, Keegan, also saw the little girl on the second floor. The child was sitting on the edge of the bed in Room 4 with her legs crossed and her chin resting on her hands. "She just looked up at me and smiled. She was so beautiful," Keegan said.

Keegan described the entire experience as peaceful and warm. "I never saw her again, but I can sense that she's

Murphy's Lamplight Inn Central Lake, MI

 still here. Every time I get a soothing or calm feeling, I know it's her," Keegan said.

A psychic who recently visited Murphy's Lamplight Inn also saw the little girl. The psychic said the child stayed here a lot with her parents and that she had a funny walk as if she had polio.

An old photo, [perhaps from the 1900's or 1910's] found under an antique wash basin on the main staircase, shows a little girl with long, dark curly hair. A family friend who saw the little girl ghost says it is the same child.

This photo is now displayed on the wall of the main staircase. It was purchased by Mary Ellen Murphy, the owner, from an antique dealer whose brother used to own the property.

Murphy's Lamplight Inn   Central Lake, MI

Research is ongoing to find out the name of the child in the photo. As of the time of printing, nothing has been found. Perhaps you recognize this photo. Maybe it matches a photo you have in an old family album.

Murphy's Lamplight Inn   Central Lake, MI

Just Stop It!

A few years ago Shana, the owner's daughter, was home visiting from college. Not really having her own room, she was staying in Room 3. It was winter time and she had gotten herself all tucked into bed. She was warm and cozy and just about to doze off to sleep when the bedroom door, which was closed, starting shaking really fast.

Irritated, she took off the covers, got out of bed and walked over to the door, but before she could touch the door handle, the shaking stopped. Shana figured she had stepped on a floorboard that stopped whatever was making the noise. So she went back to bed.

A few minutes later, just as she got warm and comfortable, the door started shaking again. So she took off the covers and went to get up, but before her feet could even touch the floor, the noise stopped.

She got back into bed and just as she got the covers over her, the rattling started up again. Now, fuming mad, she flung off the covers, but before she could sit up, it stopped. "It's like it knew I was going to

Murphy's Lamplight Inn   Central Lake, MI

get out of bed, so it better stop," she thought. "It's something that a little kid would to do to get attention."

She yelled, "Just stop it!" It stopped and she was finally able to go to sleep. The next morning she told her mother, "I'm never sleeping in that room again!"

Could it have been the little girl who was playing with the door in the hallway? Room 3 is also on the second floor.

Murphy's Lamplight Inn   Central Lake, MI

Bathroom Occupied

For years guests and workers alike have avoided the second-floor bathroom. Some wouldn't use it all, opting instead for a long and uncomfortable ride home. Others have run out of the bathroom saying, "There's somebody in there. You can't see them, but someone's there."

A psychic said the mysterious spirit's name was Roy and that he had been a traveling pharmaceutical salesman who had frequented the hotel in the 1940's. A war veteran, he self-medicated to deal with back pain, and eventually he became addicted.

Figuring his addiction made him useless to his family, he ended up leaving his wife when she was pregnant with their 8th child. Guilt ridden, he remains here as a way of avoiding having to answer to a higher power. "We all have to own up to what we did in life," the psychic said.

Murphy's Lamplight Inn   Central Lake, MI

In the 1940's, the second-floor bathroom was a hotel room.

Holly Hotel
Holly, Michigan

hollyhotel.com   **(248) 634-5208**

History

Built in 1863, the Washington House was the first building to occupy the corner where the Holly Hotel now stands. It was a modest two-story wooden boarding house. By the late 1800's, more than 25 trains a day brought visitors and settlers alike to Holly, and it was clear a bigger and more upscale hotel was needed.

Holly Hotel

John Hirst opened the massive Hirst Hotel in 1891. An upscale establishment, it featured hot water, elegant rooms and a cosmopolitan dining room. By the early 1900's the hotel was the social hub of the Holly area. Sunday dinner at the hotel was a formal event, and afternoon tea was a must for any proper lady.

In 1912 New Yorker Joseph P. Allen purchased the property and renamed it the Holly Inn. The following year, on January 19, a huge fire almost destroyed the building. Allen rebuilt the hotel in a more modest style and dubbed it the "Allendorf Hotel," an imitation of the famed Waldorf Hotel in his native New York. Although moderate in architectural features, the interior was decorated in typical Victorian grandeur with rich woods, fine fabrics and leaded glass.

All was well for several years, and the hotel kept its property and clientele upscale and elegant. Over time, however, two world wars, the Great Depression and the elimination of sophisticated train travel caused the property to fall into disrepair. By the 1970's the property had been everything from a pizza and beer joint to a transient boarding house.

Holly Hotel

On January 19, 1978, the hotel suffered another horrific fire exactly 65 years after the first fire. Ironically, both fires happened at the same time of day, and their causes were never determined. Damage for the later fire was estimated at $550,000, and the last significant link to the 1800's was being considered for demolition.

George Kutlenios couldn't bear to have the property turned into a parking lot. So with $10,000 he and his wife Chrissy set out to purchase and rebuild the hotel to its original grandeur. Two years later, with help of records and drawings from 1891 and personal accounts from local historians, the Holly Hotel opened for business.

The Kutlenioses continue to own and operate the hotel as a fine dining establishment that features world-class food, fine wines, delectable desserts and, of course, afternoon tea. Since 1980 many have visited the Holly Hotel—some guests have never left.

Holly Hotel

The Dining Car

The Holly Hotel features a smaller dining room on the main floor called the Dining Car. It is decorated to resemble a Victorian Era first-class passenger car, complete with luggage racks, vintage bags and other train memorabilia. It is a favorite with families.

About eight years ago (1999), Kim, a waitress, was doing some spring cleaning in the Dining Car. She took down all the bags, dusted and rearranged things a bit. As she started putting all the luggage back on the shelves, a luggage tag popped out from the inside of one of the bags. What was so unusual was that the address on the bag was her current address.

Initially she was taken aback by this bizarre coincidence. Then she remembered that she currently lives in an older home, where many antiques for the hotel were purchased. "What an interesting little tidbit," she thought. When she shared her story with her colleagues, "Everyone got a kick out of it," she said.

The very next day Christine, another waitress, was walking by the dining car and saw someone sitting at the table right

39

below where Kim had seen her address displayed. She thought she saw a woman
sitting there in a long white dress, who
turned her head as Christine walked by.

Originally, she dismissed it as another
member of the wait staff, sitting there
folding the hotel's famous white linen
napkins. This was typically done to prepare
for the busy weekend dinner crowd.
However, it was Wednesday afternoon,
and there would be no need for this.

Christine immediately went back to
the room only to find it empty. She
checked around, and no one had been in
that room all day. Could Kim's cleaning a
day earlier have stirred up something?

**Christine saw the woman sitting
in the corner of the Dining Car.**

Holly Hotel   **Holly, MI**

A year later a customer brought her little grandson to the hotel for dinner in the Dining Car. The grandmother bragged about how her grandson was gifted. She said with a straight face, "He's clairvoyant. He sees things all the time!"

Christine thought, "Yeah right!" but, being a good waitress, she played along. She asked the little boy, "Do you see any spirits in this room right now?"

The boy replied, "Yes, there's a lady right over there." He pointed right underneath the luggage with Kim's address on it and to the exact seat that Christine had seen the lady in a white dress a year earlier.

Second-floor Friends

Although the Holly Hotel is currently a fine dining restaurant, years ago it served as a hotel. Near the turn of the last century, Nora Kane, who was believed to be the innkeeper at the time, lived at the hotel along with her family. Sometime during her employment, it is said that she had a young daughter that passed away unexpectedly.

This portrait of Nora Kane, who is wearing a black mourning dress, hangs in the lobby.

In more recent years chefs often report that after they have closed the kitchen, they would come in the next morning and find all their pots and pans on the floor. "It wasn't that they fell down. Someone placed them on the floor," the chefs replied.

For decades, workers and guests have reported hearing giggling and the sounds of children running through the halls and up and down the staircase. This was unusual as before the hotel was rebuilt in the 1970's, it was run down and frequented by questionable clientele, therefore completely inappropriate for children.

Nowadays, some of the Holly Hotel's customers are children. They come with their families for lunch or dinner. Afternoon tea is popular with little girls, who attend with their mothers or grandmothers.

Highchairs line the wall where giggling and running is heard.

Holly Hotel

Last spring (2007) a grandmother brought her 10-year-old grandson to dinner to celebrate his good report card. After eating, the boy went to the men's room on the second floor.

When he returned to the table, he said, "I saw my spirit friend in the bathroom."

His grandmother and the waitress, wide eyed, immediately asked, "Well, what do you mean?"

He said when he exited the stall in the bathroom, there was a man standing there. Describing him as a really nice guy, the boy continued, "He wanted to come back to the table with me, but I told him he had to stay here."

Two months later a 5- or 6-year-old girl was having dinner with her family. She kept leaving the table to go upstairs to the bathroom. "She must have gone six times," the waitress noticed.

Her mother asked her if everything was all right. The child replied, "There's two little girl ghosts in the bathroom. They're my friends, and I want to go back up there and talk to them."

No Rest in the Restroom

Before the Kutlenioses rebuilt the hotel, the entire second floor was a boarding house with many bedrooms. Currently, it boasts banquet halls, restrooms and countless antiques.

For 10 years many men have dashed out of the men's room on the second floor completely terrified. These were not men prone to making up stories or drinking too much but upstanding, quiet and respectable types. They all had the same gaunt look on their faces and had the same shocking story.

The second-floor restrooms occupy the same space as the old boarding house bedrooms.

Holly Hotel   Holly, MI

While in the room, they could sense someone there. It was a gentle female presence who "spoke without using words," the men said. Telepathically, she communicated kind and comforting feelings.

Then things turned 180 degrees. Suddenly, her caring ways changed into those that were scary and ill willed. "It just made you feel really bad and afraid," they said. It made them almost run out of the room. After telling their stories to Chrissy, the owner, none of these men have used that bathroom since.

The Griffon
Lake Michigan

lasalle-griffon.org

History

The Great Lakes were formed during the last ice age from melting glacier ice. Native Americans, and later European settlers, used the lakes for much needed transportation of goods and services. Established routes began to take shape, and trading flourished.

The Griffon   Lake Michigan

The first European vessel to sail the upper Great Lakes was the Griffon, built by the famous French explorer Rene-Robert Sieur De er LaSalle as a trading vessel. The Griffon left from Washington Island (near Wisconsin) in 1679 for its return maiden voyage. It sank and has never been found.

Flash forward to modern times, and most of the boat traffic on the Great Lakes is recreational. In fact, Michigan boasts more freshwater coastline than any other state. Ask any MetroDetroiter about "Up North" and you'll likely hear a great summertime story about Lake Michigan or Lake Huron.

Little Traverse Bay in Northern Lake Michigan.

49

A Perfect Day

In the summer of 1983, a group of out-of-state vacationers set sail near the islands off the tip of Escanaba, Michigan. Two went diving, the other, Kathie, stayed on the boat to enjoy a beautifully calm, sunny day on the lake.

It was one of those perfect summer days, the kind that Michiganders dream about most of the year. It was dry and sunny; the temperature neared 80°, and there was barely a cloud in the sky. Kathie drifted off to sleep on deck.

With the warm sun getting a little too hot on her face, she awoke, and as she glanced out toward the expansive lake, a ship came into view. Not just any ship, it was a grand sailing vessel, something that Columbus would have sailed to the New World. Full color and full scale, it dipped heavily up and down in the waves, except there were no waves that afternoon—it was an utterly calm day.

The vision lasted only a few precious seconds before vanishing, but Kathie knew she had just witnessed something special. Feeling privileged to view something so

The Griffon   Lake Michigan

unexpected, unexplained and unbelievable, it was some time before she told her husband or friends about the ship.

Finally, she shared her experience. She described to the group a tall ship with sails drawn. Not being an expert on ancient seagoing vessels, she said it was a Spanish Galleon, like a pirate ship. Her husband believed her but was skeptical about it being a Spanish Galleon as they are more associated with the Florida coast than the Great Lakes.

With everyone's curiosity piqued, Kathie's husband showed her a book on European sailing vessels and asked her to pick which one most closely resembled what she had seen. She picked out LaSalle's Griffon, which is believed to have sunk in Lake Huron—or did it?

Drawing of The Griffon circa 1679.

In Search of The Griffon

Many have searched for the Griffon in Lake Huron but never in Lake Michigan. The reason for this is that historical writings from Frenchman Father Hennepin state that the Griffon sank near the Huron islands. Searchers took that to mean the islands in Lake Huron. But one modern-day diver had a different thought on where to find the Griffon.

Steve Libert, an archeological diver/enthusiast, says that the French word Huron also means "rough" or "wicked." This opens the possibility that the Griffon may have sunk in Lake Michigan near the Garden Islands. This is closer to where Father Hennepin stated the Griffon began its return journey to Niagara, Canada.

In fact, Libert has found a shipwreck [that he believes could very well be the Griffon] near the same Lake Michigan Islands. Ironically, this is the same area where Kathie saw her ship nearly 20 years earlier.

Here Comes Uncle Sam

So what's stopping Libert's group from confirming the ship's identity and salvaging the wreck—bureaucratic red tape and lots of it. The legal wranglings have been going on since 2001 and show no sign of ending anytime soon.

In a nut shell, here is the problem: Once an ancient shipwreck is identified, the country of origin can claim it. In this case the French have been cooperative and stand ready to claim the vessel. In order to identify the ship, the country and state of the wreck's resting place must give permission to begin the process.

The State of Michigan will not issue a salvage permit unless they get an exact location. Libert's group can provide this as long as the State signs a nondisclosure (to keep the public from pillaging the site) and noncompete (to keep the State from stealing the group's historical discovery).

"This has little to do with money and more to do with principle," Libert said. The Griffon is an important historical find, he explained. Contrary to what most people think, the Griffon wasn't loaded with gold or silver—it was a fur-trading vessel.

The Griffon   Lake Michigan

Hundreds of years ago, fur was like money, and although commoners could live without gold or silver, they couldn't live without warm clothes and blankets. Libert continued, "If I was looking for riches, I'd be down in Florida hunting for gold bullion with everybody else."

"The ship is a time capsule that will fill the missing gaps of LaSalle's early exploration of North America," Libert said. Although LaSalle made history for his exploration west of the Mississippi, little is known of his earlier travels.

For more details on the Griffon, legal updates and how you can help straighten out this mess, go to lasalle-griffon.org.

The Lake Michigan coastal town of Charlevoix, MI, is the host of The LaSalle-Griffon Project, 2006-2008.

National House Inn
Marshall, Michigan

nationalhouseinn.com   **(269) 781-7374**

History

The National House Inn was built in 1835 by Colonel Andrew Mann. It provided a much needed halfway retreat for travelers on the dusty stagecoach trail between Detroit and Chicago.

In 1844 the Michigan Central Railroad opened, and for the next 30 years the inn was a successful train station hotel. By 1878 the addition of dining and pullman sleeper cars eliminated the need for train depot

National House Inn   Marshall, MI

lodging, and the hotel closed. The building was converted to a windmill and a wagon factory.

Around the same time that the railroad hotel was closed, the property became part of the Underground Railroad system that helped slaves escape from the South to the North and to Canada. Artifacts found in a cave-like structure behind a basement wall have recently confirmed the inn's Underground Railroad status.

This hole in the basement wall once led to part of the Underground Railroad that linked the inn via underground tunnels with two other nearby buildings.

National House Inn   Marshall, MI

In 1902 the property was purchased by Dr. Dean, a local veterinarian, who turned it into eight luxury apartments. Over the next 75 years, Dean's Flats, as it was called, gradually fell into disrepair. By the 1970's it was clear that something needed to be done.

As a bicentennial gift to the community, restorationists Norm and Kathryn Kinney proposed returning the property to its original purpose—a quaint country inn. With the help of volunteers and a lot of hard work, the National House Inn reopened for business as a bed & breakfast on Thanksgiving Day of 1976.

The current owners continue to maintain and renovate the inn while preserving its original 18th century appeal. The inn boasts many original architectural features, countless antiques and, perhaps, a few other things left over from a time gone by.

National House Inn   Marshall, MI

Mirror, Mirror on the Wall

In 1983 the National House Inn innkeeper, Barbara, was extremely busy one afternoon doing room checks. She hurried from room to room on the second floor making sure everything was ready for arriving guests.

As she raced back and forth in the upstairs hallway, something stopped her dead in her tracks. Although she was alone in the hallway, she had the distinct feeling that someone or something else was there with her.

Wide eyed, she slowly turned around and looked down the narrow hallway—It was empty. Then she gazed into the mirror behind her. Although she saw nothing out of the ordinary in the reflection, the feeling persisted. "Something just wasn't right with that mirror. It just made me feel so uncomfortable," she said.

She immediately took the mirror down and replaced it with a picture. "I just wouldn't be able to concentrate on anything else unless I took that mirror down," she said.

The mirror that hung at the end of this hall has been in storage for nearly 20 years.

National House Inn   Marshall, MI

Little Jason

In the early 1990's the innkeeper Barbara was busy in the dining room tending to the breakfast crowd. Many guests were still enjoying their meal, and others were checking out. A young couple who had been staying at the Inn all weekend had finished eating and wanted to speak to the manager.

Barbara, who is always focused on customer service, hurried over to them wondering what could be wrong. Maybe they had a problem with their room, she thought.

It turns out that their room was fine, but they wanted to know why everyone here had been ignoring Jason for the past 30 years.

"Jason? Who's Jason?" Barbara asked.

The wife said sternly, "He's the little boy ghost that we've been hanging out with all weekend. Can't you see him? He's sitting on the stairs right now."

Barbara was absolutely stunned. She turned and looked at the staircase. She saw nothing, but the couple insisted he was there.

National House Inn   Marshall, MI

   Over the years Barbara had heard
stories of doors being opened and shut,
lights being turned on and off, but it all
seemed like harmless tales. Could Jason be
responsible for all these seemingly
unrelated pranks, she thought to herself.

   At a loss for an explanation, Barbara
apologized to the couple and promised to
stop ignoring Jason, whatever that meant.
The couple never returned. Although no
one else has ever admitted to seeing
Jason, lights still mysteriously come on,
doors open and close and unexplained
noises are still heard throughout the
building.

**Jason was seen sitting on this staircase,
which is near the main entrance.**

National House Inn   Marshall, MI

Lady in Red

Starting in the 1970's, a rumor began circulating that a Lady in Red haunts the second floor hallway. As the story goes, she was a prostitute that entertained clients from the nearby truck stop. No one knows how she died, but it is said that she is seen in the windows on the second floor.

Contrary to the story, Dean's Flats, as the property was called then, although run down was never a house of ill repute. Inn Keeper Barbara thinks the story started as a result of the building being in such bad shape. "When a property is almost abandoned, is in ill condition and basically looks haunted, people start talking and making their own assumptions," Barbara said.

Although this story has never been substantiated, Barbara and her employees have grown to embrace their Lady-in-Red urban legend. In fact, every Halloween the story is retold to an enthusiastic audience that usually includes local media. A mannequin, dressed in red, is placed in the window for all to see. "It's all in fun!" Barbara said.

Perry Hotel
Petoskey, Michigan

staffords.com   **800-737-1899**

History

The year was 1899, and northern Michigan was a comfortable place for people to escape from the summer heat. The Grand Rapids and Indiana Railroads brought settlers and vacationers to "the land of the million dollar sunsets." They all wanted a proper place to stay, dine and socialize.

Dr. Norman J. Perry gave up his dental practice (after the death of a patient during a multiple tooth extraction)

Perry Hotel   Petoskey, MI

and built the Perry Hotel. Featuring sturdy brick construction, his property was billed as the only fireproof hotel in town. This was an important attribute at a time when most buildings were wooden structures with gas lights. This was not a good combination, and many buildings perished.

In 1919 the hotel was purchased by the Drs. John and George Reycraft for use as a hospital. The city fathers disagreed, convincing them there was a need for a year-round hotel. The doctors hired their nephew Herbert Reycraft to oversee the property along with Herbert's wife Hazel. The Reycrafts doubled the hotel's capacity and added attractions like a small orchestra and weekly dances.

In 1961 the Reycrafts retired, and John Davis became the new proprietor. He changed the name to the Perry-Davis Hotel and added the panoramic window before selling to Alan Gornick in the 70's.

The current owners, Stafford's Hospitality, purchased the hotel in 1989. The entire property was restored to its original grandeur including the hotel's stamped tin ceiling, parts of the Terrazzo flooring and

Perry Hotel   Petoskey, MI

the entire wood bannister on the main stairway.

In 1900 there were 21 Petoskey area hotels in operation. Today only the Perry Hotel remains, along with a fascinating history, great memories and a few guests that checked in but never checked out.

Perry Hotel   **Petoskey, MI**

A Cool Breeze

   Northern Michigan has long been a summer retreat for Detroiters seeking near perfect temperatures and dry sunny days. However, on occasion sweltering humidity can set in, making the air thick and still. This was the case during David's first summer as rooms manager at the Perry Hotel.

   He was sitting alone at his computer in the basement near where the old hotel laundry was located, desperately trying to finish a report. With his deadline looming and the heat making it difficult to concentrate, he asked for help from a rather unlikely source.

   For years David had heard the hotel was haunted, but he never had any experiences of his own. That was about to change. He smirked, with his head in his hands, "Dr. Perry [the hotel's original owner], if you're here, please give me a hand. I need to get this done."

   Just then the box fan in the corner started blowing, creating a welcomed breeze. Although David didn't remember turning on the fan, he figured it was some kind of electrical short causing a delayed power surge.

Perry Hotel   Petoskey, MI

The circulating air made him more comfortable, and he was able to finish his work. After shutting down his computer, he went to turn off the fan, which was not only off but completely unplugged.

Shocked, he stood there with the unattached cord in his hand searching for an explanation. He had been alone the entire time. Stone faced, he quietly thanked Dr. Perry, just in case, and darted home.

Although there's still an office near the gift shop, it's now a business center for guests.

Perry Hotel   **Petoskey, MI**

100 Years Old

In the spring of 1999, the Perry Hotel was celebrating its 100-year anniversary. History presentations, tours and parties filled the calendar. Hotel staff prepared for a busier-than-usual summer season.

One afternoon a housekeeper working in the oldest part of the hotel called the rooms manager David, and said, "Could you come up here, please? You need to see this."

When David arrived, he found the housekeeper staring at the digital alarm clock, which was counting backwards. He immediately unplugged it and plugged it back in, but the clock continued its countdown.

Having seen too many movies, he secretly wondered, "Could it be a bomb?" Well, in any case, he thought, it needs to be replaced. Another clock was brought up from storage, plugged in and showed no abnormalities.

David took the old clock down to his office and, feeling a bit like an undercover spy, took it apart—just in case. Nothing seemed out of place, just your run-of-the-mill clock parts. After putting it back together, he plugged it in again only to have it continue counting backwards right where it left off. Bizarre, he thought, but not life threatening.

Having averted "danger," he needed to get back to work. So he threw a towel over the clock and left it on a shelf to deal with on another less hectic day.

Two weeks later the same housekeeper asked, "Whatever happened to that backwards clock?" Together they unwrapped the old clock, which was still plugged in. The countdown had stopped and it read "1899," which isn't even a real time of day, but it is the same year the hotel opened—exactly 100 years earlier.

By the time David got his camera, to document the strange reading, the clock was flashing 12:00.

Perry Hotel

Petoskey, MI

Ungentleman-like Conduct

The Perry Hotel boasts a well-known pub, *The Noggin Room,* located in the lower level. It features more than 30 beers from around the world. Those completing the world beer tour can add their name to the bar's famous "Hall of Foam." It is a unique gathering place with a fun atmosphere and live entertainment.

One evening bar staff noticed one of the hotel guests, a well-dressed man, had been drinking heavily and flirting with the ladies. Friendly and good looking, he had little trouble convincing women to come back to his room, which was in the oldest part of the hotel.

The man stayed in one of the Imperial rooms on the third floor.

Perry Hotel   Petoskey, MI

Due to his late-night cavorting, the breakfast crew was surprised to see him sitting in a chair outside the dining room just before 6:00 the next morning. Completely awake, showered and dressed in a coat and tie, he anxiously told one of the waiters that he wanted "A 'to go' coffee and muffin" and that he needed to leave "Immediately."

The guest was acting so strangely that the staff kept asking what was wrong. Finally, with a shaky voice he stammered,

> In the middle of the night I felt something brush my face. At first I thought it was a bug or something. Then it happened again. When I opened my eyes, I saw a lady floating above my bed. She had long flowing hair and a long white nightgown. Not knowing what else to do or say, I asked her what she wanted. With a dirty look on her face, she waved her finger disapprovingly right at me, then pointed toward the door. She wanted me to leave. And that's exactly what I did.

Perry Hotel   Petoskey, MI

Too freaked out to do anything but leave, the man had vacated his room in the middle of the night and had been waiting for the dining room to open for several hours. After getting his "to go" bag, he hurried out the door, never to return.

The staff dubbed the ghost "Lady of the Lake" (Lake Michigan is just steps away from the hotel). Men of the pub, beware; like many women from days gone by, she doesn't appreciate ungentleman-like conduct.

The Storm

Petoskey, Michigan, is no stranger to harsh weather, so when a fall storm hit in November 2005, no one thought anything of it. This was no ordinary storm; high winds, snow and freezing temperatures served as warning to everyone that the coming winter would be long and cold.

It was 3 am, and a large gust of wind blew out a window in the library on the third floor of the hotel. The wind was blowing with such force that the night manager was unable to open the door to assess the damage. After calling the manager David at home for help, the two of them finally pried open the door.

The room was freezing cold as snow continued to blow in from the outside. Shards of glass covered the chair beneath the window. Using a tarp, staple gun, knife and cutting board from the kitchen, the pair quickly mended the window until workmen could be called.

Too tired to do anymore, David hung a "closed" sign on the door and went home. The night auditor headed back to his duties, which included monitoring the hotel's many surveillance cameras. The

The green door survived the winter storm and is in surprisingly good shape.

cameras help the staff monitor public areas of the hotel, including the library.

Within a few minutes the library camera showed a woman in a white nightgown walking into the library, grabbing a book and sitting down on the chair beneath the busted window. Knowing that the chair was covered with broken glass and fearing for the woman's safety, the night manager called the phone in the library. When no one answered, he ran upstairs. The door was still closed. He pushed his way in only to find the room just as he and David had left it.

Relieved, although confused, he headed back downstairs and rechecked the monitors. The same woman was still there—It was as if she had never left. He ran upstairs again only to find the same empty room.

Once back downstairs, he checked the surveillance system. The tape showed no one in the library, yet according to the live camera, she was still sitting on the glass-covered chair. "The Lady of the Lake" didn't move and stayed on the monitor until the sun came up—two hours later.

The window has been replaced, but the same chair remains.

More Library Visitors

A year later (fall 2006), a self-proclaimed spiritual medium, along with several female students, visited the hotel. Being a gracious host, David happily showed them around the property but didn't tell them anything specific. A bit skeptical, he wanted to see what the group could pick up on, if anything. "I'll test them a little," he thought.

When the group entered the library, the medium said, "Someone just pinched me [on her butt]." David, who was the last one in the room, raised his hands in the air and said, "Wasn't me!" Everyone laughed, and the mood lightened.

Just then the medium said, "Someone wants me to do something." She closed her eyes, went over to the bookshelf, grabbed a book, walked to the chair beneath the now repaired window, and sat down. She opened her eyes and said, "I have no idea why I just did that."

Finally, A Name

By spring of 2007, some curious hotel guests wanted to hear the hotel's ghost stories. Once again David obliged and recounted the "Lady of the Lake" stories. Fascinated, they spent most of the evening in the library, reading and playing cards.

Disappointed that the "Lady of the Lake" did not make an appearance, they made one last-ditch effort to contact her. Before retiring for the evening, they asked her, "Just tell us your name." Silence followed so they headed off to their room.

The next morning when they returned to the library, there was a book sitting on the chair beneath the window where the "Lady" was last seen. The book was the *Autobiography of Doris Day*.

A month later two kids staying at the hotel also wanted to hear the ghost stories, so David repeated the stories and took them to the library. He couldn't remember what book was found on the chair a month earlier. All he recalled was that it was a woman's name that started with a "D." Convinced that his memory would be jarred if they found the book, the trio scoured the shelves for 15 minutes.

Perry Hotel   Petoskey, MI

Needing to get back to work and not wanting to leave the kids unattended in the library, David said, "I have an idea. How about we push the books back as far as we can in the shelf, and in the morning we'll check to see if any are popped out." David quickly pushed all the books in as the kids followed checking his work. Just then one of the kids said, "Wait! You forgot to push this book in!" The book sticking out was the *Autobiography of Doris Day*.

"Doris-that's it!" David said. The kids were so excited, they shouted, "The Lady of the Lake's name is Doris!" Trying to play it cool in front of the kids, David didn't let on how shocked he was. He didn't even see the book so hadn't left it sticking out.

The books in the Library are organized by color. The *Autobiography of Doris Day* is in the blue section.

Perry Hotel   Petoskey, MI

Just two months before "Doris" made her name known, the Perry Hotel bought an antique dresser from a local couple who had found it inside an old school house they had recently purchased. Inside the dresser was stamped "Perry Hotel Room 24" along with the date "2/14/1899." Could this original piece of "Perry" furniture be the reason Doris has returned?

The dresser is on display in the hallway on the second floor.

Research to find out who Doris was is ongoing. As of the time of printing, nothing has been found. Perhaps you know who Doris was? A grandmother, an aunt, or an old family friend who frequented the Perry Hotel many years ago.

Baldwin Theatre

Royal Oak, Michigan

stagecrafters.org   **415 South Lafayette**
Royal Oak, MI 48067

History

On June 22, 1922, the quarter-million-dollar Baldwin Theatre opened its doors in downtown Royal Oak, Michigan. Dubbed "the most beautiful playhouse in the state," it featured more than 1,000 seats, a pipe organ and a symphony orchestra. Silent films and vaudeville shows filled the marquee.

In an unusual business move in 1929, the owner of the Baldwin and the owners

Baldwin Theatre   Royal Oak, MI

of its rival, the nearby Royal Theater, switched properties. The deal included the stipulation that the Royal could not operate as a theater for 10 years. The Royal never reopened as a theater, and since then has housed many different businesses.

In 1936 the new owners remodeled the Baldwin and changed its name to the Washington Theater. Silent films gave way to "talkies," and eventually full-length movies ruled the screen. Over the years the building gradually fell into disrepair and closed in the early 80's. A fire in 1984 caused major damage to the vacant property.

The unique timing of the fire saved lives and the theater itself. According to newspaper reports, had the fire gone on much longer it would have consumed the entire wood structure. On the other hand, if firefighters had arrived any earlier, many lives would have been at risk from falling stage equipment like heavy lighting rigs and large scenery panels as their securing ropes burned through.

In 1985 the City of Royal Oak agreed to provide a low-interest federal loan of $125,000 to Stagecrafters, a nonprofit

Baldwin Theatre   Royal Oak, MI

theater troupe from the nearby city of Clawson. The group used the funds to renovate the entire building, including dividing it into two separate theaters for simultaneous live productions.

The theater's name was changed back to the Baldwin, and for the past 20 years, and counting, it has hosted hundreds of plays and musicals. The Stagecrafters organization is proud of its theater's past and looks forward to its future filled with entertaining productions, interesting stories and, according to some, a few unexplained ones.

Baldwin History Bibliography:
Royal Oak Public Library, Royal Oak, MI, Historical Collection/Theaters:

Daily Tribune [Royal Oak],
        June 9 & 15, 1922.
Daily Tribune [Royal Oak],
        June 13, 1984.
Daily Tribune [Royal Oak],
        February 23, 1985.

Keep it Down!

In 1991 Doug had only been volun-
teering with Stagecrafters for about a year
when he was working on an upcoming
musical. The performances were going
well, and the cast was a friendly, fun and
outgoing group, so much so that the noise
from the green room, show biz for break
room, was getting really loud even during
live shows.

After a matinee performance Doug
put up signs in the green room reminding
everyone to keep their voices down during
the show. Being a nice guy, his signs were
meant to be more humorous than rule
based. They read, "Keep quiet! Uncle Sam
says this means you!" He wanted to be
funny but still get his point across.

After putting up the last of his 10 or so
signs, he went up to the lobby. When he
returned to the green room 10 minutes
later, all of the furniture had been pushed
into the center of the room. His signs were
taken down off the walls and placed on
the pile of tables and chairs.

Doug's first thought was that the
cleaning crew must have been in the
room. Undaunted, he had some business

to finish in the light booth, so he headed upstairs. He returned a few minutes later and all of the furniture was back where it belonged, and all of his signs were back on the walls. "Wow, that crew is fast, and quiet," he thought to himself. "I never heard or saw anyone."

The next day he complimented the service crew manager. "Your crew is fast! I couldn't believe how quickly they cleaned the green room yesterday!" Doug declared.

The crew manager had a puzzled looked on his face. He said, "Ah, Doug, I didn't have a crew working yesterday."

Doug was without explanation. "No one else would have the need to move the furniture or the strength required to push all the heavy benches and tables," he thought to himself. "It didn't really scare me, but it was definitely freaky!" he said.

Baldwin Theatre   **Royal Oak, MI**

Who Moved the Boxes?

In 1998 longtime Stagecrafters volunteer Scott was working with the youth theater division for an upcoming musical production. Late one night he and another worker were the only two in the building. Scott was up in the costume room and his colleague was on the stage at the other end of the building doing some electrical maintenance work.

The costume room is located at the very top row of seats in the far left corner of the theater. It is an odd-shaped room with a tall ceiling perfect for storing hundreds of elaborate costumes. No one enjoys spending a lot of time alone in the room. "It's a very isolated place to be. All the fabric from the costumes absorbs any sound so it's very quiet—too quiet," Scott said.

Even though the room made him a bit uncomfortable, he was determined to find all the costumes and accessories he needed. Eventually he found what he was looking for and began stacking the large boxes outside the door. He stacked them in such a way that they blocked the aisle.

Baldwin Theatre   Royal Oak, MI

Having done enough for one night, he turned off the lights in the prop room and closed the door. As he turned around to pick up the boxes, they were nowhere to be found. He looked behind the many rows of seats and down the aisle, but they simply weren't there.

Scott thought maybe his coworker, or perhaps someone else who arrived while he was in the prop room moved the boxes, so he shouted, "Anyone here?" No one answered. He walked down the aisle and yelled to his colleague, who was engrossed in his electrical work, "Did you move the boxes by the prop room door?"

His colleague answered, "No."

Confused and tired, Scott went home. All night he kept wondering what happened to those boxes. Over the years, he heard whisperings of how the theater is haunted, but he had never had any personal experiences-until now.

Early the next morning Scott arrived back at the theater and found all of his boxes stacked right in front of the costume room door just as he remembered leaving them. "There's no way I could have gotten out of the room and down the steps without tripping over the boxes," he said.

A tall step leads to the costume room door.

Baldwin Theatre   Royal Oak, MI

Behind the Curtain

In the fall of 2002, Scott was asked to step in as director of an upcoming Christmas play. Although the production was already a few weeks into rehearsals, he happily accepted this new assignment. His responsibilities included everything from managing cast rehearsals to set design.

After the cast and crew left for the evening, Scott was alone doing some last-minute odd jobs. With the stage finally vacant, he thought it would be a good time to pin together the holes in the old stage curtain.

With safety pins in hand, Scott climbed up on the scaffolding and began pulling and pinning. Just then he heard someone walking below him behind the curtain. "Footsteps on the wooden stage floor make a very distinct sound," Scott said. "You could even hear them echoing throughout the theater."

Assuming somebody was there and concerned that an unauthorized person was inside the building, he slowly and quietly crept down the ladder. "I didn't want to scare whoever it was and, just in case it was an intruder, I wanted to have the element of surprise," Scott said.

Once reaching the floor, he quickly pulled the curtain back. No one was there. Convinced someone was playing a joke on him, he turned on every light in the place and checked behind each row for the culprit. He was completely alone.

After calming himself down, he went back up on the scaffolding to finish his work. As soon as he resumed what he was doing, the footsteps started up again. This time he wasn't fooling around. He jumped down off the ladder and yelled, "Come on! This isn't funny!" Silence followed.

Now Scott had a chill up his spine and felt not only was someone watching him but that the "person" didn't want him there. He has had unexplained experiences in the theater before, with boxes being moved (see previous story) and once he was firmly tapped on the shoulder while leaning against a wall, but this was different.

The experience gave him an uneasy feeling. "It was like someone knows all about you, but you don't know who they are or where they are," Scott said. He stopped what he was doing and left the

Baldwin Theatre   Royal Oak, MI

theater immediately. Nowadays when Scott has to work alone, he always has all the lights on and music playing.

The stage floor was completely replaced in the summer of 2002 before fall rehearsals started.

Please note: The above stories are the individuals' opinions and are not necessarily those of the Stagecrafters organization.

Map

About the Author

Sandy Arno Lyons was born & raised in Michigan & has lived in many cities throughout the state, including Livonia, Novi, Oscoda, Big Rapids, East Lansing, Wixom & Royal Oak. Currently she lives in Berkley with her husband. She is a figure skating coach and freelance writer.

To purchase additional copies, future editions or to check for upcoming titles, go to www.skaterightpublishing.com.